Darfur and Beyond

What Is Needed to Prevent Mass Atrocities

Lee Feinstein

CSR NO. 22, JANUARY 2007
COUNCIL ON FOREIGN RELATIONS

Founded in 1921, the Council on Foreign Relations is an independent, national membership organization and a nonpartisan center for scholars dedicated to producing and disseminating ideas so that individual and corporate members, as well as policymakers, journalists, students, and interested citizens in the United States and other countries, can better understand the world and the foreign policy choices facing the United States and other governments. The Council does this by convening meetings; conducting a wide-ranging Studies program; publishing *Foreign Affairs*, the preeminent journal covering international affairs and U.S. foreign policy; maintaining a diverse membership; sponsoring Independent Task Forces and Special Reports; and providing up-to-date information about the world and U.S. foreign policy on the Council's website, www.cfr.org.

Council Special Reports (CSRs) are concise policy briefs, produced to provide a rapid response to a developing crisis or contribute to the public's understanding of current policy dilemmas. CSRs are written by individual authors—who may be Council fellows or acknowledged experts from outside the institution—in consultation with an advisory committee, and typically take sixty days or less from inception to publication. The committee serves as a sounding board and provides feedback on a draft report. It usually meets twice—once before a draft is written and once again when there is a draft for review; however, advisory committee members, unlike Task Force members, are not asked to sign off on the report or to otherwise endorse it. Once published, CSRs are posted on the Council's website.

For further information about the Council or this Special Report, please write to the Council on Foreign Relations, 58 East 68th Street, New York, NY 10021, or call the Communications office at 212-434-9400. Visit our website at CFR.org.

CONTENTS

Foreword	v
Acknowledgments	vii
Council Special Report	1
Introduction and Overview	3
State Sovereignty and Atrocities	6
The Responsibility to Protect	9
The United Nations	14
The United States	25
Regional Organizations	31
The Responsibility to Protect and Darfur	38
Conclusion	48
Further Reading	49
Advisory Board Members	52
About the Author	53

FOREWORD

A lot has been said about the need to take action to stop and prevent mass atrocities. But less has been done. States continue to engage in mass atrocities, in part because they believe it will be tolerated by the rest of the world. Other states tend to acquiesce because they do not perceive their national interests are at stake. Finding a workable way out of this cycle is not simply a matter of scruples; it is also a matter of security. State failure and genocide can lead to destabilizing refugee flows and create openings for terrorism to take root.

Recent history is, in fact, somewhat mixed. NATO's intervention in Kosovo was an example where a number of governments chose to stop ethnic cleansing and genocide. By contrast, the mass killing in Rwanda a decade ago and now in Darfur, Sudan, demonstrate the high price of judging sovereignty to be supreme and thus doing little to prevent the slaughter of innocents.

Senior Fellow Lee Feinstein points to the UN's acceptance of the notion that sovereignty may need to be compromised when a government is unable or unwilling to provide for the basic needs of those within its state borders. The challenge for the United States and the international community is to translate this principle into practice. To that end, this report recommends that the new UN secretary-general take genocide prevention as a mission statement and mandate, and place it at the center of his and his organization's agenda. The report also makes a number of recommendations for the United States and others to build a sustainable capacity for genocide prevention that is substantial enough to deal with inevitable crises, but sustainable given other national security demands. Feinstein makes a strong case that this is doable—that is, if the international community is prepared to do it.

Richard N. Haass
President
Council on Foreign Relations
January 2007

ACKNOWLEDGMENTS

This report has benefited from the advice and dedication of a diverse and constructively critical Advisory Board. I thank each of its members, listed at the end of this report, and am flattered that they found time to devote to this project. Edward C. Luck served as chairman, and was characteristically generous in sharing his unsurpassed knowledge of the United Nations. Kenneth Anderson, Jean Bethke Elshstain, Morton H. Halperin, Joshua Muravchik, Diane Orentlicher, Samantha Power, Anya Schmemann, Peter W. Singer, and James Traub provided detailed commentary and guidance for which I am especially grateful.

The National Membership of the Council on Foreign Relations provided extremely helpful feedback on an early draft of this report. I thank James A. Thomson, Elizabeth Sherwood-Randall, and David K.Y. Tang for respectively chairing discussion groups in Los Angeles, San Francisco, and Seattle. I also wish to thank Dan Caldwell, distinguished professor of political science at Pepperdine University, for extremely helpful comments on an early draft.

I thank the following individuals for agreeing to interviews in connection with this project: David A. Hamburg, who is leading a separate effort on the UN and genocide prevention at the request of Kofi Annan; Jane Holl Lute, UN assistant secretary-general for Peacekeeping Operations; Job C. Henning, vice president, Hicks & Associates, Inc., and adviser to the Office of the Secretary of Defense; Andrés Salazar, in the UN Office of the Special Adviser on the Prevention of Genocide; Hans Binnendijk at the National Defense University; and Nancy E. Soderberg, former Deputy U.S. Ambassador to the UN.

Tod Lindberg, editor of *Policy Review*, sparked some of the ideas in this paper, as did an impromptu lunch with a new Council colleague, Michael J. Gerson, who worked assiduously on these issues at the White House. I also thank senior fellows Princeton Lyman and William Nash for their expertise, which was offered at various stages of this project.

I had the privilege of working for Speaker Newt Gingrich and Senator George J. Mitchell in 2005. Many of the ideas in this report grew out of their report to Congress, *American Interests and UN Reform.* I am indebted to them for that opportunity. My thanks also to the Council's former president, Leslie H. Gelb, and former director of Studies, James M. Lindsay, who helped crystallize my thinking on this report.

I thank the Better World Fund and its president, Senator Timothy E. Wirth and executive director, Deborah Derrick, for generously supporting this project, which evolved beyond its original scope, and Johanna Mendelson-Forman, now at the United States Institute of Peace.

Lindsay Workman read an early version of this paper and, as always, offered valued expertise and insight. I am grateful for the diligence and precision of former colleague Daniel Keegan, who helped get this project off to a fine start. Research Associate Erica De Bruin has worked hard and effectively to help bring this project to fruition. I also wish to thank my dedicated Council colleagues, Irina Faskianos, Lisa Shields, and Patricia Dorff for their hard work and support.

I thank Council President Richard N. Haass and Director of Studies Gary Samore for their scholarship and support of this project. Finally, there would be no discussion of the responsibility to protect without the pioneering work of Gareth Evans, who has been and continues to be the driving force behind this important principle.

Lee Feinstein

COUNCIL SPECIAL REPORT

INTRODUCTION AND OVERVIEW

The killing and destruction of national, ethnic, racial, or religious groups is a historical reality. So, too, is the dependable failure of the rest of the world to do much about it.

Slow-motion ethnic cleansing in western Sudan is the most recent case of a state supporting mass atrocity and the rest of the world avoiding efforts to end the killing. Preventing and stopping such mass atrocities faces four reinforcing problems.

First and most fundamentally, states of different cultures and economic circumstances continue to pursue ethnic cleansing as a national security strategy. Second, prevailing international rules and practices have been a bar to international action, and an excuse not to respond in cases where states do not believe their national interests are at stake. Third, international capacity to act, especially regional capacity, is limited and ad hoc, a function of poor planning and deliberate political choices. Finally, public support to take action to prevent mass atrocities is episodic or nonexistent, the result and product of a historic lack of political leadership around the world, including in the United States.

The profound changes in international security of the last few years, and the related changes in how and what states view as security dangers, have the potential to erode some of these barriers. One year ago the 191 members of the United Nations formally endorsed a principle known as the "responsibility to protect." The responsibility to protect is the idea that mass atrocities that take place in one state are the concern of all states. The universal adoption of this principle at the United Nations World Summit in 2005 went relatively unnoticed. Yet the adoption of the responsibility to protect is a turning point in how states define their rights and responsibilities, and removes some of the classic excuses for doing nothing.

The UN's role in averting mass atrocities is also being examined, as part of a broader rethink of the UN's purposes triggered by the Security Council crisis over Iraq in 2003. This reexamination has generated reports and investigations, and some improvement. The new secretary-general, Ban Ki-moon, needs to connect management reform to a set of clear mandates for the organization that corresponds to the world's expectations for the institution. Management reform detached from a clear assessment of the purposes of the UN is destined to sputter and fail. The new secretary-general should build a reform program that is designed to implement the responsibility to protect to begin to translate the principle into practice. Doing so would also fortify the overall push for reforms, which has faltered.

The United States and other capable states and organizations have given a degree of rhetorical support to the atrocity prevention mission. Yet, Washington and others have not enacted a policy to support their moral claims or to advance the overlapping security interest in preventing state failure, which can create the conditions that make genocide and other atrocities more likely.

Addressing the lack of political leadership in the United States and internationally is a complex and difficult issue. Public support to take action in Darfur, for example, spans a broad ideological spectrum in the United States. Yet most Americans, embittered by the Iraq experience and wary of humanitarian intervention, are skeptical that international action of any kind can be effective. That said, the public seems to support playing a more active role in Darfur, including military action and support by NATO.[1]

Overcoming these structural impediments to action requires balancing effectiveness against expense. Genocide is a historical fact and a present danger. It is possible to identify with a degree of accuracy *where* it might occur and in general terms *that* it is going to occur. But it is not possible to say exactly *when* it will happen or what will precipitate a genuine emergency. For example, there was a thirty-five-year backdrop to the 1994 slaughter of Tutsis by Hutus in and around Rwanda. This history alerted the world to the chronic danger of genocide in the region. It also dulled it to the acuity of the crisis in the weeks leading up to the killings in April 1994.

The failure to intervene militarily in Rwanda and the frustration over inaction to the stop mass killing in Darfur has had the unhelpful effect of framing the issue of

---

[1] A recent Zogby survey found that 70% of the public supports the U.S. implementation of a no-fly zone over Darfur to prevent aerial attacks on civilians. Additionally, 62% of Americans agree that the U.S. "has a responsibility to help stop the killing in the Darfur region," and 58% believe more can be done diplomatically in order to help end the crisis in Sudan. The broad support among Americans for action in Sudan is consistent with findings observed in previous polls by the Program on International Policy Attitudes (PIPA). In 2005, a PIPA survey revealed that a majority of the public (71%) supported NATO and U.S. involvement in Sudan by providing assistance to the African Union peacekeeping force in Darfur. See http://www.globalsolutions.org/programs/glob_engage/news/Zogby_poll_march06.html, http://www.worldpublicopinion.org/pipa/articles/brafricara/71.php?nid=&id=&pnt=71&lb=bthr, and http://www.worldpublicopinion.org/pipa/articles/btjusticehuman_rightsra/110.php?nid=&id=&pnt=110&lb=bthr.

preventing atrocities around the question of whether to "send in the Marines." Forcible humanitarian intervention cannot be ruled out. Nor can it be held out only as a last resort. Yet, the inherent risks of military interventions should limit invasion and occupation to extreme cases. In most instances, political, diplomatic, and a range of military options short of war are preferable and more effective.

STATE SOVEREIGNTY AND ATROCITIES

Changes in norms and legal obligations have only an indirect effect on how states behave, but they matter. Genocide has been outlawed by treaty since 1948, but mass atrocities have continued with regularity since then, accounting for as many as 20 million deaths in twenty-nine countries over the past fifty years.[2]

Yet the profound changes in international security of the last few years have changed expectations in many parts of the world.[3] These changes have roots dating back to the Enlightenment. In recent years they have been driven by the genocides of the 1990s and the perceived incompatibility of the existing legal framework with the need to take action.

The case in point is NATO's seventy-eight-day air war against the former Yugoslavia in 1999 to prevent the slaughter of Kosovar Albanians. Post-colonial states and others concerned about American motivations considered the NATO action an illegal intervention into the "domestic jurisdiction" of a state.[4] So did the overwhelming majority of international lawyers working for Western governments, who generally concluded that the action was technically illegal, even if justified, because it was not formally a war of self-defense and was not authorized by the UN Security Council.

That interpretation was wrong at the time, but it reflected the prevailing view. The State Department offered a wide-ranging justification for the Kosovo intervention, exemplifying its discomfort with the legal issues involved, and a fear of setting an international precedent that could boomerang.[5] Then President Bill Clinton did not give a

---

[2] The "Convention on the Prevention and Punishment of the Crime of Genocide" was adopted by the UN General Assembly December 9, 1948, entered into force January 12, 1951, and was ratified by the United States November 25, 1988. Available at http://www.unhchr.ch/html/menu3/b/p_genoci.htm.

[3] World Bank, *World Bank Group Work in Low-Income Countries under Stress: A Task Force Report* (Washington, DC: World Bank, 2002). Twenty-six of the World Bank's designated "low-income countries under stress" are in sub-Saharan Africa.

[4] Charter of the United Nations, Chapter I, Article II. Available at http://www.un.org/aboutun/charter/.

[5] U.S. Department of State, "Fact Sheet: U.S. and NATO Objectives and Interests in Kosovo," Washington, DC, March 26, 1999, available at http://www.state.gov/www/regions/eur/fs_990326_ksvobjectives.html; Madeleine K. Albright, "Press Conference on Kosovo," October 8, 1998. Available at http://secretary.state.gov/www/statements/1998/981008.html.

speech that was drafted for him by his staff that outlined factors for humanitarian intervention.[6]

British Prime Minister Tony Blair and UN Secretary-General Kofi Annan, however, each sought to address the question more directly. Blair's foreign secretary, Robin Cook, proposed talks among the permanent members of the Security Council on factors for humanitarian intervention. The United States stalled and ultimately rejected the idea.[7] Blair laid out his own set of criteria in an important 1999 speech in Chicago.[8]

Genocides Since 1955

Afghanistan	Chile	Iran	Sri Lanka
Algeria	China	Iraq	Sudan
Angola	D.R. Congo (Zaire)	Nigeria	Syria
Argentina	El Salvador	Pakistan	Uganda
Bosnia	Equatorial Guinea	Philippines	Yugoslavia
Burma (Myanmar)	Ethiopia	Rwanda	
Burundi	Guatemala	Somalia	
Cambodia	Indonesia	South Vietnam	

Source: Barbara Harff, "Assessing Risks of Genocide and Politicide," in Monty G. Marshall and Ted Robert Gurr, eds., *Peace and Conflict 2005* (College Park, MD: Center for International Development and Conflict Management, 2005). This list was originally compiled by Barbara Harff for the State Failure/Political Instability Task Force, a group of scholars commissioned by the CIA in 1994 to investigate the causes of state failure. It includes countries with incidents of genocide or politically motivated mass killings, which the task force terms "politicides."

Annan asked the Security Council and the General Assembly to address the issue.[9] They initially declined to do so. An international group of diplomats and experts assembled by

---

[6] Author's notes.

[7] Author's notes.

[8] Tony Blair, "Doctrine of the International Community," speech presented at the Economic Club of Chicago, Chicago, IL, April 24, 1999. Blair's five criteria include the "certainty" that military intervention is required; whether all diplomatic options have been exhausted; sufficient military "capacity" to do the job; strong international "commitment" to maintain ground troops as long as necessary; and what "national interest" is at stake.

[9] Kofi A. Annan, "Secretary-General's Annual Report to the General Assembly," September 20, 1999, available at http://www.un.org/news/Press/docs/1999/19900920.sgsm7136.html; and *'We the Peoples': The Role of the United Nations in the 21st Century, Millennium Report of the Secretary-General of the United Nations*, presented on April 3, 2000, and available at http://www.un.org/millennium/sg/report/.

Canada, however, comprehensively addressed the subject, coining the phrase the "responsibility to protect."[10] Their findings, issued on September 10, 2001, were overwhelmed by the al-Qaeda attacks the next day and it seemed this principle would be relegated to the status of a well-intentioned period piece born of a forgotten time of relative international calm.

So it is surprising that four years later, and with little fanfare, the General Assembly of the United Nations, and the Security Council the following May, would endorse the principle, with active support of much of Africa and with the backing of the United States, which had also come to support the idea.

---

[10] International Commission on Intervention and State Sovereignty (ICISS), *The Responsibility to Protect* (Ottawa: International Development Research Center, 2001).

THE RESPONSIBILITY TO PROTECT

The responsibility to protect is an idea that has migrated from policy journal to policymaking over the space of a few years.[11] The responsibility to protect has two parts. The first element of the responsibility to protect is the most important. It goes to the basic obligations of states toward those living within their borders. Andrea Bartoli, a scholar-practitioner at Columbia University, has put it simply and effectively in an imperative to states: "Don't do genocide."[12] The UN General Assembly put it more formally in its "Outcome Document" adopted by the World Summit last year:

> Each individual State has the responsibility to protect its populations from genocide, war crimes, ethnic cleansing, and crimes against humanity. This responsibility entails the prevention of such crimes, including their incitement, through appropriate and necessary means. We accept that responsibility and will act in accordance with it.[13]

The second element of the responsibility to protect goes to the responsibility of the rest of the world when a state fails to address the risk of mass atrocities within its own borders or is itself the source of the threat. The General Assembly described this duty comprehensively:

> The international community through the United Nations also has the responsibility to use appropriate diplomatic, humanitarian, and other peaceful means, in accordance with Chapters VI and VIII of the Charter, to help protect populations from genocide, war crimes, ethnic cleansing, and crimes against humanity. In this context, we are prepared to take collective action, in a timely

---

[11] Roberta Cohen and Francis M. Deng addressed this issue extensively in the period following the Rwandan genocide, concluding, "A government that allows its citizens to suffer in a vacuum of responsibility for moral leadership cannot claim sovereignty in an effort to keep the outside world from stepping in to offer protection and assistance." See Roberta Cohen and Francis M. Deng, "Normative Framework of Sovereignty," in Deng et al., *Sovereignty as Responsibility: Conflict Management in Africa* (Washington, DC, Brookings Institution Press, 1996). The International Commission of Intervention and State Sovereignty (ICISS) coined the phrase "responsibility to protect" in 2001. In addition to the endorsement of the General Assembly and the Security Council, the principle was endorsed by the UN secretary-general in 2005, the High-level Panel on Threats, Challenges and Change in 2004, and by Newt Gingrich and George Mitchell in their congressionally mandated task force report, *American Interests and UN Reform*, on which the author served as an expert and the principal author.

[12] Telephone interview with Andrea Bartoli, director, Center for International Conflict Resolution, Columbia University, March 9, 2006.

[13] UN General Assembly, Sixtieth Session, *2005 World Summit Outcome*, A/RES/60/1, 2005, para. 138.

and decisive manner, through the Security Council, in accordance with the Charter, including Chapter VII, on a case-by-case basis and in cooperation with relevant regional organizations as appropriate, should peaceful means be inadequate and national authorities manifestly fail to protect their populations from genocide, war crimes, ethnic cleansing, and crimes against humanity.[14]

The responsibility to protect redefines sovereignty. Its adoption is a watershed, marking the end of a 350-year period in which the inviolability of borders and the monopoly of force within one's own borders were sovereignty's formal hallmarks. Instead, the responsibility to protect says that sovereignty entails rights as well as responsibilities. The extent to which a state enjoys the full benefits of sovereignty is a condition of its behavior.

The significance for preventing mass atrocities is clear. First, the United Nations has skirted Talmudic debates about whether an atrocity is genocide by concluding that international action is warranted for a range of actions even if they do not meet a formal definition of genocide.

Second, the endorsement of the responsibility to protect by the General Assembly—and by the Security Council the following May—places "genocide, war crimes, ethnic cleansing, and crimes against humanity" on par with other threats to international peace and security. Adoption of the responsibility to protect begins to resolve the historic tension between human rights and states' rights in favor of the individual. Where the state had been erected to protect the individual from outsiders, the responsibility to protect erects a fallback where individuals have a claim to seek assistance from outsiders in order to substitute for or protect them from the state.

The responsibility to protect places individual citizens and their most basic human right—as the Declaration of Independence says, "the right to life"—at the center of the international system. In doing so, the responsibility to protect erodes the classic rationale for inaction, namely that intervention to prevent mass atrocities constitutes illegal interference in the sovereign affairs of a UN member.[15]

These are important words, but in the end only words. In light of their potentially controversial consequences, however, their staying power is surprising, and important.

---

[14] Ibid., para. 139.

[15] The following analysis has informed my own: Tod Lindberg, "Protect the People," *The Washington Times,* September 27, 2005.

Sovereignty has always been less than absolute in reality. What is it about the world today that generated the idea that sovereignty should be seen as less than absolute in theoretical and legal terms as well?

Part of the answer rests in how states perceive threats in the current security environment. In particular, the 9/11 attacks reinforced a "failed-state" analysis of security dangers that is congenial with the trend to define sovereignty in conditional rather than absolute terms.[16]

The al-Qaeda attacks on the United States also vividly demonstrated how the means of mass destruction are no longer the monopoly of states. In a world where catastrophic terrorism is more than a theory, the trend has been to frown on self-help, even if the cause is valid. As an example, the United States has supported efforts to revive international negotiations on a Comprehensive Convention on International Terrorism. The main impediment to concluding the treaty has been disagreement about how to define terrorism. After 9/11, however, a consensus developed to define it broadly. The High-level Panel on Threats, Challenges and Change, a group appointed by Kofi Annan, for example, called on states to adopt the following definition:

> Any action...intended to cause death or serious bodily harm to civilians or non-combatants, when the purpose of such act, by its nature or context, is to intimidate a population, or to compel a Government or an international organization to do or to abstain from doing any act.

It added, "There is nothing in the fact of occupation that justifies the targeting and killing of civilians."[17] The United States has supported this approach. In calling for conclusion of the terrorism convention, President George W. Bush told the UN General Assembly in 2005 that he supported putting "every nation on record that targeting and deliberate killing by terrorists of civilians and noncombatants cannot be justified or legitimized by any cause or grievance."[18]

If the preference is to discourage self-help because of the risk of terrorist intervention or unintended consequences, then there has to be some other process by

---

[16] White House, *National Security Strategy of the United States of America*, September 2002.

[17] Secretary-General's High-level Panel on Threats, Challenges and Change, *A More Secure World: Our Shared Responsibility* (New York: United Nations, December 2004), pp. 51–52.

[18] George W. Bush, "Address to 2005 World Summit High Level Plenary Meeting," speech given at the United Nations, September 14, 2005.

which grave humanitarian grievances can be addressed. In a setting where redress by non-state actors is restricted or discouraged, the responsibility to protect is more than a moral doctrine; it is an important pillar of the international system.

LIMITS OF IMPLEMENTATION

Agreeing on the principle of the responsibility to protect is not the same thing as acting on it. The inherent political barriers to implementing the responsibility to protect can delay urgent assistance, inject helpful precaution, or something in between.

The responsibility to protect is limited in what it can accomplish. First and foremost is the inescapable fact that the principle will not be applied uniformly. Inevitably, the decision to take action—political, diplomatic, or otherwise—will reflect the realities of power and circumstance. This is especially true where, having run out of options short of force, some form of military action appears warranted. Rather than lament the inevitable unevenness of application, the report of the International Commission on Intervention and State Sovereignty (ICISS) embeds it in a series of "precautionary criteria" for action, including, in the case of a military response, the "reasonable prospect" that it will succeed. As the report says, "It will be the case that some human beings simply cannot be rescued except at unacceptable cost—perhaps of a larger regional conflagration, involving major military powers. In such cases, however painful the reality, coercive military action is no longer justified."[19]

Another risk of the responsibility to protect is that it will be used as a basis for other exceptions to the presumption against intervention. The reality, however, is that states going to war have historically found plenty of comfort in claiming "self-defense," and do not need new justifications.

Who decides on whether to take action, when, and what kind is a more serious problem. The Security Council is the preferred place to authorize action but the permanent five members have not prioritized atrocity prevention, and have other competing claims that interfere with humanitarian goals. China and Russia joined last

---

[19] ICISS, *The Responsibility to Protect*, p. 37.

year's consensus in support of the responsibility to protect but have expressed opposition to the doctrine since then, at least in part because they fear it will be used as a political weapon against them. China has also used its opposition to humanitarian intervention to win influence in parts of the developing world where intervention, humanitarian or otherwise, is still associated with colonialism or proxy Cold War interventions.[20]

In light of changing international expectations about state responsibility and humanitarian protection, China might be expected to calibrate its positions. Yet, Beijing has played the major role in blocking strong Security Council action against the government of Sudan for its complicity in mass killings in Darfur, where attacks by the Khartoum government, its proxies, and rebel groups have led to more than 200,000 deaths and displaced nearly 3 million people. China, however, has not faced much criticism, or any tangible consequences, for its role in protecting Sudan. How Beijing would resolve competing claims if it felt genuine international pressure is an untested proposition.

The lack of actual capacity—diplomatic, military, and otherwise—reinforces the political barriers to early and effective action. While it is not possible to create a new system in toto, the goal is to build up capacity so that when there is a political opportunity to act it can be applied. The hope is that over time this will be self-reinforcing. The place to start is with the United Nations, whose program of reforms so far has produced mixed results.

---

[20] The sway of the traditional anti-interventionists, however, is not as great as it once was, as expansion of the ranks of democracies in Africa and in the United Nations more generally has eroded nonaligned movement solidarity on this issue. Since the Rwandan genocide, progressive African states have emerged as ardent supporters of the responsibility to protect. The African Union's charter, concluded in 2000, specifically addresses genocide and other war crimes in its mandate.

THE UNITED NATIONS

The new secretary-general of the United Nations, Ban Ki-moon, inherits an institution that is grappling with demands from the United States and other major contributors for "reform."

When the U.S. Congress contemplates UN reform, it tends to focus on managerial reforms, call them reforms with a small *r*.[21] These go to such issues as whistle-blowing protection, establishment of an independent audit function, and sunsetting provisions for General Assembly mandates, which, until now, have continued in perpetuity. A recent scorecard shows progress on management reforms within the UN Secretariat's domain, where the secretary-general can take action on his own initiative.[22] To the degree that the overall pace of reform is discouraging, which it is, it is probably better than efforts to modernize the State Department, which has more resources and fewer political constraints.[23] Overall, the UN's spotty record is consistent with the structural limitations of change in a universal organization of 192 members.

But a more profound rethinking of the UN's role in light of changed international conditions is a higher priority. Call this uppercase "Reform." This kind of evaluation goes to new priorities for the United Nations in light of the security transformations of the past few years, and the profound differences in the UN's role today from its intended role at its founding sixty-one years ago. Management reform detached from a clear assessment of the purposes of the UN is not only uninteresting, it is also destined to fail. The new secretary-general should build a reform program that is designed to implement the responsibility to protect to begin to translate the principle into practice.

---

[21] Enlargement of the Security Council is, of course, a separate issue, which was addressed only in passing in the various reports produced in the past three years.

[22] Better World Campaign, "Progress on United Nations Reform Based on U.S. Priorities," July 13, 2006. Available at http://www.betterworldcampaign.org/pdf/Progress_UNReform.pdf.

[23] James Dobbins has compared U.S. progress in peacekeeping with UN progress, but no one has done a comparison of reform of the State Department and the UN.

At present the UN's genocide prevention efforts are focused on the Office of the Special Adviser for the Prevention of Genocide, established by Annan in July 2004, ten years after the Rwandan genocide. The purpose of the office is to put a specific focus on genocide in light of the UN's failure to act in Rwanda and the former Yugoslavia. The office has a mandate that includes collecting information, providing early warning, making recommendations to the Security Council on steps to prevent genocide, and coordinating with other parts of the UN. In his first two years on the job, the part-time head of the office, Juan Mendez, has traveled to Darfur twice, and reported on the ethnic character of attacks against foreigners in Côte d'Ivoire. In October 2005, the special adviser's request to brief the Security Council about his trip to Darfur was blocked by the United States, China, Algeria, and Russia, despite requests from Annan and the eleven other members of the Security Council to allow it. U.S. Permanent Representative John Bolton said he objected to the briefing, asking, "How many officials from the secretariat does it take to give a briefing?"

A reform program oriented around the responsibility to protect would leverage the capabilities of this new office, and the broad range of UN capacity, from the Security Council to the Office of the High Commissioner for Human Rights to the Department of Peacekeeping Operations. The goal is to build a sustainable program that operates like an insurance policy. The policy would have to be substantial enough to meet challenges during the times when crisis threatens but does not develop and strong enough to address emergencies when they happen. The policy would be buttressed by monitoring and mitigation measures, plus an emergency capacity to respond to crises.

Monitoring

Early warning is a favorite topic for policymakers interested in genocide prevention. In truth, there is already a well-developed literature that identifies conditions that pose a risk of mass atrocity. The CIA, for example, has developed a watch list based on a range of factors, and excellent nongovernmental sources exist as well. The Office of the Special Adviser is charged with providing information about states where the risk of genocide or mass atrocities is greatest. But his staff of two is unable to do this on its own. In addition, the decision to investigate a state or region is politically freighted and subject to political pressure within the UN system.

Mitigation

The responsibility to protect is often mistakenly understood to be a doctrine governing the use of military force for humanitarian protection. It is not. The responsibility to protect, instead, implies a responsibility of the broader international community to "react" when states are unwilling or unable to protect those living within their borders from grave harm.[24] The international action that is implied can be political, diplomatic, economic, or military. The ICISS emphasized that forceful humanitarian intervention should only be considered in "extreme and exceptional cases," which it defined as "cases of violence which…genuinely 'shock the conscience of mankind,' or which present…a clear and present danger to international security."[25]

In truth, options that fall well short of force are almost always preferable. They are politically easier to initiate and sustain, they avoid the inherent risks of war, and they can often be more effective, especially if pursued early and shrewdly.[26]

The most effective actions, in fact, may be those undertaken cooperatively, with the government of concern, rather than against it. The United Nations has relevant capacity to "assist" governments in a broad range of areas, including building more effective judicial systems and law enforcement, demobilization of combatants, short- and long-term economic assistance, and human rights education and training. The Office of the Special Adviser for the Prevention of Genocide has initiated a study to identify the specific types of assistance that might be provided. The advantage of a cooperative approach is that it sends a clear message to the state of concern by setting an expectation of proper behavior. A state's response to offers of assistance would give a clearer indication of state complicity and, if necessary, build a case for more robust international action later. Offers of assistance open doors to states and to the international community to act within states.

When a cooperative approach does not sufficiently mitigate the risk of mass atrocities, international action, including the threat or application of sanctions, may be appropriate. Sanctions fall into three broad categories: political and diplomatic, economic, and military. Sanctions that target leadership groups, individuals, and organizations have emerged as an increasingly important alternative to the blunt instrument of broad-gauge sanctions.

Political and diplomatic measures might include restricting or limiting diplomatic representation. They may include restrictions or the threat of restrictions on travel,

---

[24] ICISS, p. 29.
[25] ICISS, p. 31.
[26] Richard N. Haass and Meghan L. O'Sullivan, eds., *Honey and Vinegar: Incentives, Sanctions, and Foreign Policy* (Washington, DC: Brookings Institution Press, 2000).

particularly against specific leaders and their families. Suspending a government's membership in an international or regional body is another option. The African Union (AU), for example, suspended two states in 2005 (Mauritania and Togo) after attempts to overthrow democratically elected governments. The threat of legal action against individuals and leaders responsible for war crimes is another effective policy tool.

Economic sanctions might include targeting the foreign assets of a country, rebel movement, or terrorist group, or the foreign assets of a particular leader, including members of his or her family. Restrictions on income-generating activities, such as oil, diamonds, logging, and drugs, are another important type of targeted sanction because it is often easier to get at the activities than at the hidden funds they generate.

Military measures can include ending military cooperation or military training; arms embargoes on weapons, ammunition, or spare parts; military cooperation with regional organizations or neighboring armies; preventive military deployments to stanch the spread of a civil conflict; enforcement of no-fly zones; and naval blockades, among many others.

RESPONSE

In extreme cases, or to stabilize a situation after a peace is established, some kind of military action may be needed. There is a range of military options, many of which do not involve shooting.[27] The kind of military intervention will depend on the objective and the circumstance.

The far end of the spectrum is "forcible humanitarian intervention." The UN Security Council may be asked to authorize such military interventions, but the United Nations is itself unsuited to conduct them, and they are appropriately shunned by its Department of Peacekeeping Operations. The difficulty and inherent risks of high-intensity combat operations generally require leadership by a single nation, militarily

---

[27] Richard N. Haass, *Intervention: The Use of American Military Force in the Post-Cold War World* (Washington, DC: Brookings Institution Press, 1999).

competent group of nations, or regional organizations (see below), rather than a UN force.

UN operations, however, can be and are often essential to the atrocity prevention mission. There can be no exit for combat forces deployed to stop or prevent mass atrocities without competent forces to conduct stabilization and reconstruction following closely behind. This is precisely the role that UN troops filled in Kosovo, and UN troops performed a similar role in East Timor.

UN peacekeeping forces are also often deployed to stabilize a peace negotiated among conflicting parties. UN peacekeepers successfully carried out such missions in El Salvador, eastern Slavonia, Mozambique, and Namibia, and they are likely to be called on again in Darfur, Burundi, and Congo.

Other UN operations that can be relevant to the genocide prevention mission include the "preventive deployment" of troops, such as the 1995 deployment of blue-helmeted peacekeepers (mostly American) to contain the spread of war and ethnic cleansing in the Balkans, and the deployment of "interposition" forces, such as the French and UN troops sent to patrol a buffer zone between Côte d'Ivoire's warring parties in 2004.

A recent study by RAND points to the relative success of the UN in fulfilling mandates to stabilize and rebuild nations after the establishment of peace. The RAND study attributes this success to a UN effort to incorporate lessons learned into its doctrine and operations. The RAND report says the overall trend of the United Nations is ascending the learning curve, a sharp contrast, it notes, with the failing U.S. efforts in Afghanistan and Iraq.[28]

UN peacekeeping of all kinds is now experiencing an unprecedented surge, after a lull in the mid-1990s. Expansion of UN peacekeeping operations is likely to boost the number of UN-commanded troops to 100,000 in eighteen operations over the course of 2007. Only the United States has more troops deployed overseas. While UN peacekeeping operations have improved in recent years, the traumas of the 1990s continue to take their toll.

---

[28] James Dobbins, Seth G. Jones, Keith Crane, Andrew Rathmell, Brett Steele, Richard Teltschik, and Anga Timilsina, *The UN's Role in Nation Building: From the Congo to Iraq* (Santa Monica: RAND, 2005), pp. xvi–xvii, xxxi–xxxiii.

One consequence of past peacekeeping failures is that virtually all the major troop contributors to the UN's eighteen operations are from the developing world, the expanded peacekeeping operation in Lebanon notwithstanding. The five top contributors are Bangladesh, Pakistan, India, Jordan, and Nepal. The two largest financial contributors to the United Nations (the United States and Japan) have a total of forty-three troops in UN peacekeeping.[29] Even such traditional peacekeeping contributors as Canada (twenty troops) and the Netherlands (eighteen troops) have abstained from UN operations since the failures in Somalia and Bosnia, and the scars they left.

Although peacekeeping troops operate best when deployed in circumstances of relative peace and quiet, UN peacekeepers are still saddled with Security Council mandates they cannot possibly fulfill, in such places as Haiti, the Congo, and southern Lebanon. As these deployments make clear, the reality is that the Security Council has asked and will continue to ask that peacekeepers operate in much more challenging environments.

Compounding the problem is the fact that UN peacekeeping is still at the very early stages of institutionalization. UN peacekeeping headquarters is poorly staffed. Only 600 people in headquarters supervise the operations of the troops in the field.[30] UN peacekeepers are of uneven quality. The United Nations assembles forces for each new operation without any cadre of reserve professional troops to rely on. Just-in-time recruitment of troops ensures that it will take months to fulfill even urgent peacekeeping requests, and that the forces will be of uneven quality.

Yet UN peacekeepers may be the only alternative in cases when the major powers themselves are reluctant to act because they do not feel their direct interests are at stake. The perception of having a ready and capable force at the United Nations would reinforce a habit of taking action, and erode the sense of resignation that tolerates mass killing.

Recently, there has also been discussion of whether the UN could bolster its peacekeeping capacity by employing mercenaries from private military firms in certain

---

[29] The Cold War tradition of major powers staying out of peacekeeping operations is no longer offered as sufficient justification for abstaining from UN missions. On the contrary, China is often criticized for not participating more fully in peacekeeping operations, and has been ramping up its participation in recent years. India, which aspires to permanent membership, has in recent years become one of the world's largest contributors. Japan's nonparticipation is a function of its domestic constitution.

[30] This figure excludes another 3,000 military observers and 8,000 military police.

capacities. Though controversial, there are reasons to consider this proposal. Drawing on preprepared stocks of manpower and materiel, private military firms can deploy faster than the UN; with a private-sector focus on expediency and efficiency, they carry out their missions at significantly lower cost. In the past, they have provided combat assistance to countries including Angola and Sierra Leone. They can also support critical noncombat functions, such as logistics, transport, and surveillance. The private companies have serious drawbacks, however, notably the lack of an established legal framework for regulating their activities.

The enduring weakness of UN peacekeeping is the inability to field forces in sufficient numbers when it counts. The lack of a rapid response capacity is a long-standing problem, with roots dating back to the founding of the organization. Several proposals to make incremental improvements in procurement, airlift, and stockpiling of equipment are now under consideration.[31] But, as the High-level Panel on Threats, Challenges and Change said, "It is unlikely that the demand for rapid action will be met through [these] mechanisms alone."[32] What is needed, as Annan recommended, is "an interlocking system of peacekeeping capacities that will enable the United Nations to work with relevant regional organizations in predictable and reliable partnerships."[33] The European Union and the African Union have taken preliminary steps to create national forces that would be available for deployment to UN operations should they be authorized by the Security Council. There is as yet no systematic effort to broaden or coordinate this effort to include others, due to concerns of cost and accountability raised by the United States, Japan, and other major financial contributors to UN peacekeeping.

---

[31] The Department of Peacekeeping Operations is now experimenting with an effort to pre-identify troops to be on standby at home as a strategic reserve. The reserve would most likely be held by the major troop contributor to a particular operation. The reserve would be identified as part of the planning process for the operation, and called into action in the case of an emergency or unforeseen circumstance as was the case in the EU reinforcements sent into the Congo in Operation Artemis in 2003.

[32] High-level Panel, *A More Secure World*, p. 69.

[33] Annan, *In Larger Freedom*, p. 40.

- Ban Ki-moon should take the General Assembly's endorsement of the responsibility to protect as a mandate and mission statement for the UN and build a reform program that is designed to implement it.

- The United Nations should develop a set of steps that can be taken, first in cooperation with a state or group, where there is a concern about the national or ethnic character of violence. These measures should include offers of human rights training, assistance in establishing effective judicial systems and law enforcement, the dispatch of UN diplomats to resolve disputes, economic assistance, and fact-finding missions.

- The United States and the other major financial contributors to UN peacekeeping should announce their support for the establishment of a strategic reserve of forces designated by countries to be available to peacekeeping missions if the Security Council authorizes a mission. The United States should initially work through the G-8 to promote this effort. Designated troops of an international reserve force could not be deployed without a national decision to do so. Such forces would exercise with one another, and would be trained to international standards. Countries would get modest payments to prepare forces, supplemented by additional payments when and if they are called into action.

- To respond quickly and effectively to new or expanded Security Council mandates, the United States should support a proposal now before the General Assembly to create a pool of 2,500 civilians who would permanently be on call for peacekeeping missions. This would provide a cadre of trained professionals around which the Department of Peacekeeping Operations could rapidly expand or adjust to changing peacekeeping demands.[34]

- The United States should support a recommendation for the permanent Security Council members to withhold the use of the veto in the case of dire humanitarian need, except when their own vital national security interests are at stake. Such an

---

[34] The UN has estimated the annual cost at $280 million. See Kofi A. Annan, *Investing in the United Nations: For a Stronger Organization Worldwide, Report of the Secretary-General* (New York: United Nations Press, 2006).

informal agreement would remove another obstacle to early Security Council action. The Bush administration successfully blocked efforts to include this recommendation in the September 2005 UN agreement.

- The United States should support the discretionary authority of the UN Special Adviser on Genocide to brief the UN Security Council. This office should have adequate resources. The job of the special adviser should be converted into a full-time position, and additional staff should be assigned to the office to consolidate reporting functions in this office. The special adviser can minimize controversy by reporting on regions of concern in an annual report, which would provide a baseline for other investigations.

- The Geneva-based Office of the High Commissioner for Human Rights is an underutilized resource in helping to prevent and deter atrocities. High Commissioner Louise Arbour has proposed the early deployment of human rights officers to crisis situations to provide timely information and draw attention to situations requiring action. Human rights advisers may also collect information that might be helpful to future criminal prosecutions, serving also a deterrent role.

- The secretary-general and the United States should support the expansion of the mandate of the newly established Peacebuilding Commission to include a stronger pre-conflict role, including the capacity to monitor and provide recommendations on developing situations in countries that have not already faced conflict but are in danger of sliding into it.[35]

- The new Human Rights Council, whose role is to spotlight human rights abuses and shame abusers, can demonstrate its credibility if it treats the human rights records of its members without fear or favor. Members should be prepared to subject their human rights records to genuine peer review, as the new resolution recommends. Democracies on the Council must work together if the new body is to operate effectively.

---

[35] The High-level Panel recommended creating the Peacebuilding Commission to coordinate UN activities as well as the efforts of the international financial institutions, other donors, and nongovernmental organizations (NGOs) to "avoid state collapse, the slide into war, or assist a country's transition from war to peace." In the fall of 2005, the General Assembly approved a cramped version of the Peacebuilding Commission, limiting its role to post-conflict work.

- To limit micromanagement of its affairs and improve efficiency, the Department of Peacekeeping Operations and its undersecretary should operate with greater management authority while remaining politically accountable to the Security Council.

- The secretary-general should commission a panel to explore options for employing private military firms, especially for noncombat functions. It would not be necessary to rewrite international law for this purpose—instead the UN could adopt its own, voluntary regulations for contracting private military firms.

THE UNITED STATES

The Bush administration has presided over a period in which a range of Americans has expressed concern about genocide and mass atrocities. This is the product of long-standing moralistic tendencies in American foreign policy and the emergence of politically mobilized religious communities that have taken a special interest in this issue.

These moral concerns have been reinforced by changing assessments of U.S. national security priorities since 9/11. After the al-Qaeda attacks, the Bush administration adopted as its own a focus on failed and fragile states, which was earlier outlined by the Clinton administration as part of an overall globalization strategy. The Bush administration's National Security Strategy describes the need to shore up weak and failing states, on both humanitarian and counterterrorism grounds, as does the 2006 Quadrennial Defense Review (QDR), which emphasizes the importance of U.S. military efforts to "build partnership capacity" in the developing world to "inoculate societies against terrorism, insurgency, and non-state threats."[36]

President Bush has also become more concerned about U.S. policy toward atrocity prevention. During his first presidential campaign in 2000 he said, "I don't like genocide and I don't like ethnic cleansing, but I would not send our troops."[37] The following year as president he famously wrote, "Not on my watch" in the margins of a 2001 National Security Council (NSC) memorandum that described Washington's failure to lead a global effort to stanch the 1994 Rwandan genocide. In its second term, the Bush administration endorsed the responsibility to protect, and supported its adoption by the United Nations at the World Summit in negotiations during August and September of 2005.

After the failure to prepare for the rebuilding of Iraq following the 2003 invasion, the administration announced steps intended to improve the U.S. government's ability to carry out the mission of stabilization and reconstruction, tasks also essential to a capacity for atrocity prevention. The administration issued National Security Presidential

---

[36] U.S. Department of Defense, *Quadrennial Defense Review Report (QDR)*, February 6, 2006, p. 91.
[37] Interview with Sam Donaldson, ABC *News This Week*, January 23, 2000.

Directive 44 (NSPD-44) in December 2005 to create a national architecture for stability operations, giving the secretary of state interagency leadership on the issue. In August 2004, the administration created the Office of the Coordinator for Reconstruction and Stabilization at the Department of State, with an assistant-secretary level "coordinator," with a direct reporting line to the secretary of state, at its head. The office was initially conceived to "serve as a sort of Joint Chiefs of Staff for the various agencies involved."[38] The 2006 Defense Department Quadrennial Defense Review announced readiness to support UN peacekeeping operations: "The Department stands ready to increase its assistance to the United Nations Department of Peacekeeping Operations in areas of the Department's expertise, such as doctrine, training, strategic planning and management."[39] Former Secretary of Defense Donald Rumsfeld said, "If there's anything that's clear in the twenty-first century, it's that the world needs peacekeepers."[40] The Defense Department approved Defense Department Directive 3000.05 in November 2005, formally elevating the mission of stabilization and reconstruction to place it on a par with "war fighting."[41]

These reforms and policy statements are a welcome shift from earlier administration policy. The armed forces have generally taken the lead in implementation. Government-wide efforts, however, are suffering from a perceived lack of support at senior levels.

President Bush's "Not on My Watch" pledge has not been followed up with a formal strategy for implementation. Efforts by the NSC to implement NSPD-44 have hit bureaucratic roadblocks, and energy behind implementation has taken a backseat to the wars in Iraq, Afghanistan, and other higher-order national security priorities. A reorganization is under way at the State Department, raising questions about the priority given to responsibilities carried out by the Office of Reconstruction and Stabilization. The State Department has not seized opportunities to fund that office, including not taking full advantage of a provision of the fiscal 2006 Defense Authorization Bill, which

---

[38] National Defense University (NDU), "U.S. Support for UN Peacekeeping: Study on Possible Areas for Additional Assistance from the Department of Defense," October 12, 2006, p. 18.
[39] U.S. Department of Defense, *QDR*, p. 90.
[40] Quoted in NDU, "U.S. Support for UN Peacekeeping," p. 11.
[41] U.S. Department of Defense, "Directive Number 3000.05: Military Support for Stability, Security, Transition, and Reconstruction (SSTR) Operations," November 28, 2005.

gave the Secretary of Defense the discretion to give $100 million to the State Department to build institutional capacity to support reconstruction and stabilization. The United States is now $400 million behind in payments for UN peacekeeping, reversing the excellent record of the Bush administration, which until recently had caught up on UN arrears accumulated during the 1990s. Increases in operations in Darfur, Lebanon, East Timor, and the Democratic Republic of Congo are likely to deepen U.S. peacekeeping debt.

Overall, the Pentagon has gone furthest in implementation. The Defense Department's Quadrennial Defense Review calls for deeper U.S. military involvement in nation building. The QDR says the Defense Department "must become as adept at working with foreign constabularies as it is with externally focused armed forces, and as adept at working with interior ministries as it is with defense ministries—a substantial shift of emphasis."[42] In August 2006, the Pentagon proposed a significant reorganization, subject to congressional approval, of the Office of the Under Secretary of Defense for Policy. It would, among other things, establish an office for Global Security Affairs, headed by an assistant secretary of defense. The reorganization has been described as bringing a "key Defense Department office more in line with the growing emphasis on managing international military coalitions, equipping partner nations to fight terrorists, and managing the U.S. military response to a growing array of transnational threats."[43] This reorganization has the potential to intensify and better coordinate a focus on building competent indigenous forces, an opportunity enhanced by new leadership at the Army. These promising steps, however, are balanced by the military's concern that it lacks committed civilian partners, a worry reinforced by the uncertain future of stabilization and reconstruction efforts at the State Department.

Congress is divided on the issue of improving coordination of U.S. capacities to conduct stabilization and reconstruction. Senators Joseph Biden (D-DE) and Chuck Hagel (R-NE) championed the creation of the Office of Reconstruction and Stabilization at the State Department, and continue to support it. But there is resistance elsewhere. On the left is an unwillingness to give this office greater capacity as an indirect expression of

---

[42] U.S. Department of Defense, *QDR*, p. 90.
[43] "In Sweeping Overhaul, DOD Reorganizes Policy Office," *InsideDefense.com*, August 28, 2006.

disapproval of the administration's Iraq policy. On the right is long-standing disapproval of the nation-building mission on grounds that it diverts the military from its core, war-fighting mission. Public opinion exacerbates these challenges. The Iraq war has soured Americans on the muscular foreign policy they were prepared to support in the aftermath of 9/11.[44] To the degree that some kind of consensus had developed on genocide prevention, it is shallow and dissipating with every day of the Iraq war. Concern about overstretch did not translate into financial backing in the 109th Congress to support participation of other nations' troops in UN peacekeeping operations.

Recommendations

- The Bush administration should make "Not on My Watch" formal U.S. policy. It should issue a presidential decision directive that operationalizes the concept. A presidential decision directive would: identify the prevention of mass atrocities as an important national security interest of the United States, not just a humanitarian goal; outline the diplomatic and military steps the U.S. government is prepared to take; and develop a strategy for working with other leading democracies in the United Nations and with regional organizations as a foreign policy priority. The president should use the Office of Management and Budget effectively to line up support for this policy. The United States should support the proposition that a legal determination of genocide should not be necessary to trigger international action.

- Secretary of State Condoleezza Rice should develop a program to institutionalize atrocity prevention into the normal work of the State Department. To that end, she should develop a strategy, which would include a plan for working with U.S. allies and the members of the Security Council on rules of the road for international action in cases of humanitarian emergency. She should develop tailored strategies within the State Department for each of the countries that appears on the periodic CIA watch list to reduce risks in these specific cases. The secretary of state should strongly support

---

[44] Pew Research Center for the People & the Press, in association with the Council on Foreign Relations, *America's Place in the World 2005* (New York: Pew Research Center, November 2005).

the mission and activities of the Office of Reconstruction and Stabilization, lobby Congress to fully fund the activity, and invest in building an institutional capacity at the State Department for this critical mission.

- The new secretary of Defense, Robert Gates, should reaffirm support for fulfilling the recommendations of the 2005 Defense Department Directive, putting the stabilization and reconstruction mission on par with war fighting. Inadequate implementation of reforms elsewhere in the U.S. government is disappointing but does not change the importance of this mission, and is not a reason to hold back on the military's efforts to build U.S. and international capacity. With respect to U.S. forces, new leadership at the Army provides an opportunity to reinvigorate efforts to train and equip U.S. forces for the stabilization and reconstruction mission. To that end, the U.S. Army chief of staff should augment selected brigade combat teams to carry out the stabilization and reconstruction mission through added capacity, training, and doctrinal adjustments.

- The Department of Defense should fulfill the QDR commitment to support UN peacekeeping through selective participation in the UN command structure, including additional military planners at UN headquarters and at headquarter positions at UN operations in the field.

- The Department of Defense, working with the CIA and the Department of State, should develop a system of intelligence sharing that could assist the United Nations in immediate tactical needs. UN officials have said tactical intelligence could have yielded important information in UN operations in the Democratic Republic of the Congo and on the Lord's Resistance Army in Uganda. In addition to cell phone tracking information and tactical surveillance, UN officials cite the need for cartographic information.[45]

- The National Intelligence Council should resume the practice suspended in 2001 of briefing the Department of Peacekeeping Operations and Security Council representatives on current and potential conflicts in order to assist the United Nations and representatives of the Security Council with contingency planning. Officials at

---

[45] NDU, "U.S. Support for UN Peacekeeping," p. 34.

the Department of Peacekeeping Operations have requested that these strategic briefings resume.

- The United States should bring its participation in the voluntary UN Stand-By Arrangements system up to the standards of other militarily capable states, including Britain and Australia. Washington's nominal participation in the program sets a poor example for others, and does little to enhance the UN's operational capability. The United States should provide detailed information about the logistical and other support it is prepared to make available, and the United States should encourage active participation of other states.

- The White House, supported by the Congress, should support UN and international efforts to establish strategic reserves of forces designated by countries to be available for rapid deployment if authorized by the Security Council, and subject to the national decisions of each country. Forces would be trained to certain standards and take part in relevant exercises with one another. Contributing countries would receive modest payment to designate and train such forces, and a supplement when and if they are deployed. The major financial supporters of UN peacekeeping, particularly the United States and Japan, have traditionally opposed such efforts due to the expense. The unprecedented demand on America's volunteer army and on UN peacekeeping, however, should prompt a reassessment.

- The administration should request and the new Congress should support full funding for UN peacekeeping operations. The United States has voted to establish or sustain each of these missions, and in doing so, accepted a responsibility to fulfill its obligations to support them financially.

REGIONAL ORGANIZATIONS

Coalitions of militarily capable states will be a critical part in building an effective capacity to prevent mass atrocities. NATO has referred to this mission, and has operated in this capacity in Kosovo and elsewhere. The European Union and other G8 countries are building military capacities that can also be effective, though they have been silent on the specific issue of preventing genocide. The African Union's charter specifically addresses genocide and other war crimes in its mandate, and building up its capabilities will be essential.

NATO AND THE EUROPEAN UNION

NATO ministers identified in 2005 "oppression, ethnic conflict, economic distress, the collapse of political order, and the proliferation of weapons of mass destruction" as new threats requiring the organization's attention. NATO clearly has the military capacity to establish a credible capability to act against genocide. NATO's international staff sees this as a raison d'être, but the organization's most capable militaries, notably Britain and France, do not want to be in NATO's toolbox. Nonetheless, NATO has begun to build up its forces to increase its ability for humanitarian intervention. In November 2002, NATO formally created a new Response Force intended for a wide range of missions in addition to collective self-defense, including peacekeeping and peace enforcement. The force conducted its first large-scale maneuvers in Africa in the spring and summer of 2006 in Cape Verde, in an exercise comprising 7,000 air, land, and naval forces.

NATO's role in Darfur has been fairly limited so far, focusing primarily on airlifting AU troops into the region and officer training.[46] NATO and NATO states have limited capacity to deploy rapidly given other commitments in Afghanistan, the Balkans, the Congo, and in UN peacekeeping operations in southern Lebanon, Cyprus, and the

---

[46] NATO airlifted some 16,000 troops into and out of Darfur over the past eighteen months. It has provided training in operational planning to some 200 AU officers on an ad hoc basis.

Golan Heights.[47] But they can do more to increase indirect support to operations in Darfur. In addition, a number of NATO states, including Norway, Poland, and Greece, have spare capacity and could pledge troops to serve in a predominantly African force in a hybrid AU-UN mission in Darfur.

The EU's proposed response force also could be a major asset for preventing and stopping atrocities. In 1999, the EU set the goal of raising 60,000 troops that could be deployed within sixty days to carry out humanitarian, rescue, and peacekeeping operations. This effort, however, is well behind schedule. In 2000, the EU identified fifty-five distinct capability gaps—particularly in the areas of transport capacity, force protection, and integration—that needed to be resolved before a force of the envisioned size becomes operational. In December 2004, the EU agreed to a new program, called the "Headline Goals 2010," which pushed back the deadlines for the rapid reaction force and focused on creating two 1,500-person "battle groups" in the short term.

The battle group concept is promising. It builds off the experience of Operation Artemis, in which the EU sent 1,700 troops to secure a town in the Democratic Republic of Congo in 2003, enabling the return of some 60,000 refugees. This mission was the EU's first outside of Europe, and it was largely a success. Should such battle groups become operational for use in similar circumstances in the future, it would clearly be a major asset to international atrocity prevention. At the same time, the European vision of a more robust force should not be discarded. Expanding the battle group concept to a brigade-sized force would be within reasonable bounds for the short term, and it would give the EU the capacity to secure large expanses of territory in conflict zones.[48] It is also important that the EU organize these forces sooner rather than later, so as to conduct joint training exercises with potential partners. Greater EU-AU familiarity, for instance, would help ensure the interoperability of these units when they are called into combat.

---

[47] Non-U.S. NATO states are currently fielding 21,000 troops in Afghanistan, 10,000 in Iraq, 5,300 in the Balkans, 2,300 in the Congo, 5,700 in the expanded UN operation in southern Lebanon, 550 in Cyprus, and 440 in the Golan Heights.

[48] A recent study by the Center for Technology and National Security Policy at the National Defense University (NDU), for instance, argues that a brigade-sized unit would be sufficient to secure the entire area of Darfur. See David C. Gompert, Courtney Richardson, Richard L. Kugler, and Clifford H. Bernath, "Learning from Darfur: Building a Net-Capable African Force to Stop Mass Killing" (Washington, DC: National Defense University, 2005).

Recommendations

- The United States should promote formal NATO acceptance of a role in preventing genocide and mass atrocities. NATO should develop guidelines for providing support to African operations and build African capacity to conduct forcible interventions so that Africa is not wholly reliant on outside military capability to deter or defeat killing forces.

- NATO should agree to an AU request to expand training of its soldiers for the reconstruction and stabilization mission. NATO should formalize its advisory role in the African Union's operational planning by committing permanent staff to the African Union mission in Darfur and at AU headquarters. To improve mobility and communications of the African Union mission in Darfur, NATO should conduct a formal assessment of equipment needs and coordinate offers of assistance from the EU and other donors. NATO states with spare capacity, including Norway, Poland, and Greece, should pledge troops to a potential AU-UN mission in Darfur.

- The EU's Headline Goals should explicitly be pursued in order to create an EU capacity to implement the responsibility to protect. The EU should adopt the responsibility to protect as an element of its Common Security and Foreign Policy. This will reinforce the Security Council's endorsement of the principle, and create a basis for acting outside the Security Council should that prove necessary.

- The EU should continue to raise battle group units specially trained and equipped for atrocity-prevention missions, and maintain these units at a high state of readiness. The EU should build toward a brigade-sized contingent of these forces. These forces should conduct regular training exercises with partners, such as the AU, NATO, and the United States.

If outside action is necessary to avert atrocities, it is almost always preferable that it come from the region.[49] The African Union has demonstrated a willingness to play this role, despite limited military capacity and political constraints.

The founding act of the African Union, concluded in 2000, establishes "the right of the Union to intervene in a Member State pursuant to a decision of the Assembly in respect to grave circumstances, namely: war crimes, genocide and crimes against humanity."[50] In light of the experiences of the 1990s and continued economic, political, ethnic, and tribal strife, the African Union has been supportive of the responsibility to protect, and generally welcoming of Western and UN assistance to improve capabilities in the region. The African Union's philosophy is to favor "African solutions to African problems." In that regard, the Economic Community of West African States (ECOWAS) deployed 3,000 troops to Liberia in 2003. The overstretched AU force in Darfur has agreed to extend its mandate until the end of the year and increase its size from 7,200 to eleven thousand 11,000 troops.

In 2003, the African Union also approved the establishment of an African Standby Force (ASF).[51] The ASF plans to build five "regional" brigades, which would total nearly 20,000 troops by 2010. The brigades would be deployed on the authority of the AU African Assembly or Peace and Security Council. The prospective missions include peacekeeping, disarmament programs, and humanitarian relief. Development of the regional brigades is uneven. Particular weaknesses include limited command and

---

[49] As the ICISS noted, "countries within the region are more sensitive to the issues and context behind the conflict headlines, more familiar with the actors and personalities involved in the conflict, and have a greater stake in overseeing a return to peace and prosperity." See ICISS, *The Responsibility to Protect*, pp. 53–54.

[50] African Union, *Constitutive Act of the African Union*, Article 4, July 11, 2000.

[51] African Union, *Policy Framework for the Establishment of the African Standby Force and the Military Staff Committee*, adopted by African Chiefs of Defense Staff, May 15–16, 2003.

control, communication, and intelligence capabilities, substandard ground and air transportation, and a limited pool of trained and capable troops.[52]

The United States, Britain, France, and the United Nations have each taken steps to improve military capabilities within Africa. These have focused largely on building peacekeeping capacity within the region.

The Bush administration established the Global Peace Operations Initiative (GPOI) in 2004 to improve peacekeeping capabilities throughout the world, with a focus on Africa. The goal is to train 75,000 peacekeepers, primarily from Africa, over fifteen years. Under this program, its predecessor, and a similar program undertaken during the Clinton administration, Benin, Botswana, Ethiopia, Gabon, Ghana, Malawi, Mali, Mozambique, Nigeria, Senegal, South Africa, and Zambia have received U.S. peacekeeping training. In fiscal 2005, some 14,000 African troops were trained under the program, including forces that were deployed to the African Union mission in Darfur.[53]

The initiative also received the support of G-8 members at the 2004 Sea Island summit. Britain has developed a Pan-African Conflict Prevention Strategy, which includes training 17,000 African troops for peacekeeping by 2010. France is leading a separate multinational effort, called Reinforcement of African Capacity to Maintain Peace, which focuses on training units of the African Standby Force for regional peacekeeping.

The overall success of this program is difficult to gauge at this time. Standards to measure the success of the program, including the number of trained troops that participate directly in peacekeeping operations, are not publicly available. Senate appropriators have expressed concern that the State Department, which administers the program, "has failed to demonstrate a requisite level of commitment to the program, instead viewing funds provided for GPOI as a funding source for other activities."[54] A plan proposed by the 109th Congress to shift the program to an account managed by the Department of Defense would bar ten countries from participating in the program,

---

[52] Victoria K. Holt with Moira K. Shanahan, "Africa Capacity Building for Peace Operations: UN Collaboration with the African Union and ECOWAS" (Washington, DC: Henry L. Stimson Center, February 2005).
[53] Nina M. Serafino, *The Global Peace Operations Initiative: Background and Issues for Congress*, Congressional Research Service, October 3, 2006, pp 4-5.
[54] Senate Report 109-277, 109th Congress, 2d sess., pp. 91–92.

including militarily capable states within Africa such as South Africa, because they have not agreed to grant immunity to the United States for prosecution under the treaty establishing the International Criminal Court.[55]

The GPOI program has focused primarily on basic peacekeeping tasks. The capacity to conduct forcible humanitarian interventions to stop genocide, however, does not presently exist in Africa, and there is no corresponding effort to build such expeditionary combat capabilities on the continent.[56]

Developing specialized, combat-ready troops would be the most challenging element of AU capacity building. Doing this well will require close cooperation with Western militaries and developing a measure of compatibility between African and Western forces, including incorporating information technology that would make African forces "faster, better informed, more agile, and more precise and economical in their effects."[57] Such forces would have the capacity to stop killing forces, which are typically poorly trained and unmotivated. An initiative of this kind would be a deterrent to mass killings and a major asset for preventing them on the African continent.

Recommendations

- The AU should welcome and continue to solicit the support of outside nations to develop its military capacity with the goal of reducing its reliance on outside forces to prevent mass killings. The African Union cannot meet the goals of establishing five standby brigades by 2010 without substantial U.S. and NATO support.

- The United States, through the new office of Building Partnership Capacity at the Department of Defense, should conduct a formal assessment of the progress and foreign policy contribution of the GPOI program, which has yet to be subjected to a systematic evaluation. What progress is being made toward the president's goal of

[55] Serafino, *The Global Peace Operations Initiative*, p. 12.
[56] The NDU study also proposed the creation of an African Humanitarian Combat Force. This force would operate under the auspices of the African Union, as an element of the African Standby Force, with a defined mission of being available to stop mass killing. The force would rely on substantial Western assistance and direct cooperation in military interventions, particularly in the short and medium term.
[57] Gompert et al, p. 3.

training 75,000 troops, principally in Africa, by 2015? Is this the right goal? Are U.S. and international efforts growing the available pool of troops for UN and other missions and, if not, what changes are necessary? On the basis of this assessment, Western governments should adjust and intensify their commitments to bilateral training initiatives.

- The AU should continue to bring pressure to bear on regimes that fail to uphold the responsibility to protect, as it did by suspending two members last year for threatening democratically elected governments, and by denying Sudan the presidency of the organization in 2006.

THE RESPONSIBILITY TO PROTECT AND DARFUR

If Darfur is the first "test case" of the responsibility to protect, there is no point in denying that the world has failed the entry exam.[58]

BACKGROUND TO THE CONFLICT

The current conflict in Darfur began in February 2003, when the Sudan Liberation Movement, a newly formed rebel group, joined the Justice and Equality Movement in a series of attacks on government military posts. The government of Sudan responded to the provocation by mobilizing proxy militias, the Janjaweed, drawn from Darfur's indigenous Arabs. The first wave of killings began in 2003. The Sudanese army and Janjaweed developed a pattern of close counterinsurgency cooperation. Improvised bombs of "explosives and metallic debris" dumped out of the doors of Russian transport aircraft were followed closely by successive raids by attack helicopters and fighter-bombers. Janjaweed militia on camel and horseback, sometimes assisted by army units, swept in to finish the job, by burning villages, killing principally young men, and forcing survivors to flee. The displaced fled to areas sometimes protected by Sudanese police. Janjaweed patrolled the perimeters, however, attacking women and girls who left.[59] By early 2004, as many as 80,000 people had been killed as a result of the conflict, and more than 1 million displaced, including 100,000 in refugee camps outside the country.[60]

Washington and others were initially slow to recognize the carnage; the Sudanese government had begun cooperating with Washington after 9/11, and Khartoum succumbed to U.S. pressure to sign the North-South peace agreement, which ended a decades-long civil war in Sudan that claimed the lives of 2 million people. It was not until September 2004 that then-U.S. Secretary of State Colin Powell described the

---

[58] International Crisis Group (ICG), "Getting the UN into Darfur," *Africa Briefing No. 43*. Nairobi/Brussels, October 12, 2006; Joseph Loconte, "The Failure to Protect: Lessons from Darfur," *The American Interest*, Vol.2, No. 3, January/February 2007.

[59] Gérard Prunier, *Darfur: The Ambiguous Genocide* (Ithaca: Cornell University Press, 2005), p. 100.

[60] Ibid, p. 91.

conflict in Darfur as genocide and not until January 2005 that the International Commission of Inquiry, which investigated the mass killings on behalf of the United Nations, reached the softer conclusion that the Sudanese government and associated Janjaweed militias were responsible for "serious violations of international human rights and humanitarian law."

By the end of 2006, an estimated 250,000 people had died as a result of the conflict, and nearly 3 million out of a total population of 6 million Darfuris were displaced. The UN estimates that 40 percent of Darfuris now depend on outside assistance for their survival. The military situation remains precarious, despite the announcement in January 2007 of a sixty-day cease-fire. Rebels have regrouped and renamed themselves the National Redemption Front, and have renewed attacks against the Sudanese Army. Khartoum launched an offensive against rebel groups last November, accompanied by a surge in Janjaweed activity. Two major relief organizations have halted operations out of concern for the security of their staff. The UN's humanitarian chief, Jan Egeland, noted a "dramatic deterioration" in the humanitarian situation in November, saying the region has teetered "closer to the abyss than I have witnessed since my first visit in 2004."[61]

The conflict in Darfur also continues to spill into neighboring Chad, where some 200,000 refugees from the conflict have joined the 90,000 internally displaced persons uprooted by Chad's civil war. Both Chad and Sudan have accused each other of supporting rebellions in their countries.

TURNING POINT

The Darfur conflict is now at a turning point, similar to Bosnia in 1995. A pallid military force, United Nations Protection Force (UNPROFOR), did not prevent the first wave of ethnic cleansing against Muslims that began in 1992, including the massacre of 7,000 Bosnian Muslims under formal UN protection at Srebrenica. The failure of the UN effort

---

[61] Jan Egeland, "Briefing to the Security Council," UN Department of Public Information, November 22, 2006.

eventually convinced the Clinton administration to lead a NATO bombing campaign to prevent further killing. The intervention of the United States, plus ground gains by Muslim and Croat forces, proved to be the punch in the nose that got then President of Serbia Slobodan Milosevic to back down and negotiate in Dayton.

There is no guarantee that early action by the United States and others would have moderated or prevented the Darfur conflict. Yet, the regime made concessions to Washington in the past. Khartoum forced Osama bin Laden out of Sudan in 1996 under pressure from the Clinton administration. It responded to Bush administration warnings after 9/11, and agreed to provide Washington with intelligence information about its former friends. In January 2005, Khartoum concluded the Comprehensive Peace Agreement, mediated by Washington, agreeing to accept the presence of UN peacekeepers in southern Sudan. Implementation of penalties or pressure authorized in Security Council resolutions dating back to July 2004 would have sent a determined message to the government of Sudan. International support to the African Union Mission in Sudan, which has never reached its authorized troop strength, would have signaled regional commitment to the humanitarian principles of the AU Charter. Concerted U.S. diplomacy rather than deference to Beijing would have also frustrated Khartoum's efforts to expose rifts within the Security Council. Having pursued this range of options, the international community would at least have laid the basis for a stronger response down the road.

The questions for Darfur now are what kind of action is needed to prevent a potential second genocidal wave; what, if any, action could get a confident Bashir government to relent; and what are the obstacles to mustering international will to carry out an effective political-military strategy?

The responsibility to protect outlines a range of options to achieve the first two of these objectives. As discussed earlier, the responsibility to protect calls for an international response that can stop mass atrocities, war crimes, and crimes against humanity, including genocide. Responses can be political, diplomatic, economic, and military. Military responses can span the range of options from cooperative assistance to the extreme case of forcible intervention against the will of a government. The overriding theme is the priority to protect the rights of people over protecting the right of states to do as they please.

In Darfur, the immediate goal is to provide protection for the civilian population, including 2 million people dispersed in 200 refugee camps in the country, and in twelve refugee camps in eastern Chad.

The present focus, supported by the United States, is on regional diplomacy to win Khartoum's agreement for a hybrid AU-UN force, whose mission would be to protect civilians and deter destabilizing rebel attacks. UN officials say that a credible force must have "sufficient military power to deter or defeat spoilers," including surveillance and reconnaissance, a command-and-control capability, and air and ground reaction forces.[62]

Diplomatic efforts to get Sudan's agreement to an international force have failed so far, and show little prospect for success. In Addis Ababa in early November, representatives of the Khartoum government accepted a hybrid force "in principle." But Khartoum hinged its consent on reaching agreement about the size and command of the force. Despite the government of Sudan's agreement to a sixty-day cease-fire in January, Khartoum continues to say that deploying a UN force would signal a return to "colonialism," and has insisted that the force be all African with only technical support from outside. The limitations the Khartoum government wants to place on an international force would make it impossible to provide a real measure of security for the people of Darfur. Even if Khartoum consented to a credible operation, the United Nations has said it will take months to field a small advance force.

The Darfur problem is an immensely difficult one. No solution is guaranteed to work. The facts will never line up one hundred to zero. Any policy will be messy. Setting policy requires a frank understanding of the risks and choices on the basis of those risks. Freedom isn't free, and neither is protection. The hard truth is that enforcing the responsibility to protect entails risks. If the prevailing policy is zero tolerance for casualties, then enforcement of the responsibility to protect is an empty promise.

The goal then must be to craft an effective policy that carries the lowest possible costs to the people who need protection, to the regional forces that bear the brunt of the

---

[62] Kofi A. Annan, "Report of the Secretary-General on Darfur," S/2006/591, July 28, 2006, p. 16.

risk, and to U.S. and European forces acting behind the scenes. The risk of a terrorist response in the United States, Europe, or elsewhere also cannot be ruled out. Any policy also needs to weigh the risks to broader U.S. foreign policy goals, including in the Arab world, where another Western-supported military operation in the Muslim world will be viewed with disdain, whatever the facts of the Muslim-against-Muslim killing in Darfur.

Getting Khartoum's formal support for a capable peacekeeping force should remain an international goal. The linchpin to getting Sudan's agreement to a peacekeeping force may be gaining wider adherence to the Darfur Peace Agreement (DPA), which has been signed by only one of the eight splintering rebel factions. (That signatory has since been co-opted by the Bashir government, and its leader, now living in Khartoum, depends on Khartoum for protection.) There is dispute about whether an agreement is possible soon. A Western adviser to the DPA negotiations says agreement is "not a distant hope: the political differences are small." If and when there is a peace to keep, introduction of UN peacekeepers or a hybrid force "will follow."[63]

Yet, the list of broken commitments by the Bashir government is long. There are questions about whether Khartoum will accept a minimally capable international force unless there is a cost for refusing to do so. In the meantime, delaying deployment of peacekeepers prolongs the insecurity of Darfuris, who remain vulnerable to Janjaweed and government attacks.

Nothing short of a major deployment of competent troops can provide a reasonable guarantee of security, but three interim steps would improve the situation now, and would also send an overdue message of seriousness to the Bashir government.

Recommendations

Immediately Strengthen the African Union Mission in Sudan

The African Union agreed on November 30 to extend its mandate for six months until June 2007. The African Union has a mandated troop strength of 11,000 troops, yet it has fielded only 7,200 troops since early 2005. Rwanda now has 1,800 troops in the African

---

[63] Alex de Waal, "I Will Not Sign," *London Review of Books*, Vol. 28, No. 23, November 30, 2006.

Union Mission in Darfur, and Nigeria has 2,000. Each could increase its contributions significantly. African troops currently serving in the UN mission in southern Sudan can also be transferred to Darfur at acceptable risk to the 2005 North-South accord.

The United Nations, the United States, and Europe can also improve the capacity, caliber, and morale of the African Union force. A place to start is to ensure that AU troops receive a paycheck; they were unpaid for two months last summer. Among the areas where Western states could play a role is equipping reinforcements. The United States, for example, has already armed and trained Nigerian troops, and trained Senegalese and Rwandan forces. NATO has also been ferrying African Union troops inside Darfur, but the support has been ad hoc and limited. A more dedicated effort would improve the AU's responsiveness, enabling a smaller number of troops to be more effective.

NATO and the Africa Union have been engaged in a years-long routine of "After You, Alphonse." NATO defers to the perceived pride of the African Union. The African Union does not request outside support because it fears the political consequences while using NATO's reticence as the formal excuse. The United States must get an unambiguous NATO commitment to provide consistent support for the African Union, and Washington and others should press the African Union, on that basis, to accept assistance.

Ready an International Force Now

The United Nations, supported by the Permanent five members of the Security Council, should intensify efforts to identify peacekeeping troops for a prospective international operation. So far, only Bangladesh, Nigeria, and Tanzania have volunteered to put troops on the ground. Norway and Sweden have offered a small joint engineering battalion. Within Africa, capable states are waiting to see who makes the first move. Western states with available military capacity are waiting for Africans to volunteer, and also want a clearer indication from the African Union that outside support is wanted. China has been participating much more widely in UN peacekeeping operations. Pledges by China to participate in a mission in Darfur would provide some political cover to the Sudanese government to accept an international force and pressure Khartoum to do so. Beijing has privately signaled it is considering contributing troops to a blue-helmeted force.

The absence of military capacity reinforces an absence of political will. If no ready sources for a peacekeeping operation are apparent, there is no impetus to push for fast deployment. The Bashir government interprets the lack of peacekeeping forces as an expression of international division and indifference, which it exploits and uses to its own purposes.

UN peacekeeping operations are at a historical peak. NATO and the United States are pinned down in Afghanistan and Iraq. Yet if there is a sense of crisis, states find the resources to shake loose, as they did in response to the conflict in southern Lebanon last summer.[64]

Enforce the UN and DPA Flight Bans

The Security Council authorized a ban on "offensive military flights" in 2005. The Security Council has not enforced that ban. The Darfur Peace Agreement also committed the Sudanese government in 2006 to end hostile military flights, and established a still-born cease-fire commission with responsibility for enforcement and monitoring. Yet, Khartoum has continued its bombing campaign in the eight months since the agreement was concluded.

The Security Council, backed by the African Union, the United States, and the European Union, should take action to enforce the bans it authorized and Khartoum accepted. Sudan should be warned that indiscriminate air attacks against Darfuri villages or refugee camps, or attacks on rebels that create disproportionate collateral damage, will be treated as possible war crimes for referral to The Hague. Rebel groups operating in Darfur or in neighboring refugee camps would also be warned to refrain from attacks.

The warning should be issued by the widest possible group of states, preferably including the Security Council and the African Union. A diplomatic strategy would be built around the prospect of issuing the warning, including more intensive diplomacy with the African Union, the Arab League, and China. One observer has proposed a meeting of P-5 and AU ministers in Khartoum to send a much more focused signal of international concern.[65] An intensified diplomatic push should also be supported by

---

[64] France, Italy, and Germany dispatched troops quickly, speeding the initial deployment of troops to an expanded UNIFIL operation.
[65] Morton Abramowitz, "A New Tact on Darfur," *The Washington Post*, October 23, 2006.

acceleration of economic pressure on the Bashir government, including sanctions on private firms held by the Khartoum leadership.[66]

A direct way to enforce flight bans would be to destroy or disable aircraft on the ground (rather than attempting to shoot aircraft in mid-flight), relying primarily on reinforcements to the AU force, which would secure the principal air bases used by the Sudanese air force. In the event of a flight confirmed to violate the bans, forces on the ground could shut down a runway, disable, or, if necessary, destroy aircraft. Because Sudan's fleet of improvised bombers (Antonov An-12 transports), fighters, and helicopters cannot travel long distances, the number of airfields to be secured would be small. El Fashir is Sudan's main air base in Darfur. There is already a Western presence at El Fashir, which also serves as the staging area for humanitarian flights by the United Nations and others.[67]

Another option is establishing a no-fly zone over Darfur. Carrying out a no-fly zone effectively would be a difficult and costly round-the-clock operation. Stringent rules of engagement would be needed to reduce the risk of shooting down the wrong target. Even with precautions, however, it would be impossible to eliminate those risks, as past efforts over Iraq and Yugoslavia illustrate. A no-fly zone would also require reliable, probably NATO, ground troops, to identify targets and direct attacks. A no-fly zone is also likely to interrupt humanitarian flights, which are the principal lines of support to remote refugee camps inaccessible by ground. Neither of these options is without risks, but both are preferable to leaving the current population at risk. Either decision would represent a significant escalation of Western involvement and a direct challenge to Khartoum, which should only be pursued if there is the stomach in Washington and Europe for a fight.

---

[66] The ICG report, "Getting the UN into Darfur," identifies a series of economic sanctions and other penalties to pursue.

[67] Sudan lacks the capability to fly into Darfur from bases in the South, so it is possible to limit the most likely sources of attacks.

Summoning the political will to take risks is the main obstacle to converting the responsibility to protect into a program of action. Although the responsibility for atrocities against the African minority in western Sudan rests with the Khartoum government, the failure to stop the killing is a collective one.

Some have blamed the United Nations, and the presence of non-democracies on the Security Council, including veto-holding members, for the failure to apply the responsibility to protect in Darfur.[68]

The United Nations has failed to take strong action in the first instance because China has adopted the role of Sudan's protector on the Security Council. In an indication of broader hostility to an international effort in Darfur, the Human Rights Council in November narrowly rejected an EU-Canadian resolution calling on the Sudanese government to prosecute those responsible for atrocities in Darfur.

Nonetheless, the Security Council has succeeded in producing a series of resolutions on Darfur since 2003, including resolution 1706, passed August 31, 2006, which specifically connects the responsibility to protect to Darfur—the first time the Security Council invoked the principle in relation to a particular conflict. The Security Council has also authorized a ban on Sudanese military flights, referred indicted war criminals to the International Criminal Court in March 2005, and created a pathway for sanctions on certain financial interests of the Sudanese leadership.

Criticism of the United Nations is a form of self-criticism. The United Nations system was designed by its American framers not to be able to act decisively without great power consensus. Structural sloth is a built-in protection against a UN that acts without the consent of its most prominent members. These structural impediments both frustrate and serve larger U.S. interests.

Neither the United States nor the other democracies on the Council is pressing to carry out the unenforced Security Council resolutions. In the case of Darfur, the world's militarily capable and prosperous states, generally democracies, have been unwilling to take risks for a humanitarian principle that does not touch their vital national security

---

[68] See Loconte, "The Failure to Protect: Lessons from Darfur."

interests. As Newt Gingrich and George Mitchell wrote, recently, "On stopping genocide, all too often 'the United Nations failed' should actually read 'members of the United Nations blocked or undermined action by the United Nations.'"[69]

The lack of Security Council agreement on Darfur is not a legal bar to action. Even if China were now to balk, Security Council resolution 1591 gives Chapter VII authority to enforce a flight ban over Darfur, and resolutions 1672 and 1679 authorize further action on economic and political sanctions. Given the existing authority, there is no need to apply the Kosovo precedent, where the relevant regional organization, NATO, was justifiably prepared to act without express Security Council approval. In any case, the Kosovo example, reinforced by the approval of the responsibility to protect in 2005, provides a compelling precedent for action outside the UN when exigency demands. As Annan said, "The choice...must not be between Council unity and inaction in the face of genocide, as in the case of Rwanda, on the one hand; and Council division, and regional action, as in the case of Kosovo, on the other." The problem in the response to Darfur is not a lack of legal authority, but a lack of will.

The evidence of the past three years is that the world is not prepared to use force or even concerted pressure to force the government of Sudan to end its military campaign in western Sudan. In the absence of international will, Khartoum will retain the capability to act with impunity, opening the possibility of further war crimes in Darfur, and deepening the possibility that a conflict that is seeping across borders will engulf the region. The weak international response to date is discouraging. The question is whether the prospect of a second wave of atrocities will compel governments to act.

---

[69] Newt Gingrich and George Mitchell, *American Interests and UN Reform: A Report of the Congressional Task Force on the United Nations* (Washington, DC: United States Institute of Peace, 2005), p. 4.

CONCLUSION

In adopting the responsibility to protect last year, the United Nations accepted the principle that mass atrocities that take place in one state are the concern of all states. The new secretary-general should begin to bridge the gap between these words and the institution's deeds by taking the General Assembly's endorsement of the responsibility to protect as a mandate and a mission statement. Economic and militarily capable states and organizations including the United States must also take steps to bolster UN action, and to be available when the UN is not.

Darfur illustrates the difficulties in converting the principle of the responsibility to protect into a program of action. The difficulty is acute when, as in this case, the international response is slow and inadequate. The failure to demonstrate seriousness to Khartoum early has left the world with a Hobson's choice. Focusing on diplomacy now will be read by Khartoum as a permission slip to do as it pleases. Military action may be the only way to get Sudan to relent, yet it is dangerous, not guaranteed to succeed, and, as a consequence, unlikely to receive broad international political support.

The long-term goal is to avoid the stark options of "Doing Nothing" and "Sending in the Marines." That requires establishing a pattern of early and effective international response at the first signs of concern. The place to start is with concrete steps to build capacity—diplomatic, economic, legal, and military—in support of the principle of humanitarian protection. Universal adoption of the responsibility to protect has begun to remove the classical excuses for doing nothing in the face of mass atrocities. What is needed now is the capacity and political will to back it up.

FURTHER READING

Annan, Kofi A. *In Larger Freedom*. New York: United Nations, March 21, 2005.

Annan, Kofi A. "Intervention." Ditchley Foundation Lecture XXXV, June 26, 1998. Available at: http://www.ditchley.co.uk/page/173/lecture-xxxv.htm.

Akhavan, Payam. "Report on the Work of the Office of the Special Adviser of the United Nations Secretary-General on the Prevention of Genocide." *Human Rights Quarterly* 28:4, November 2006.

Binnendijk, Hans and Stuart E. Johnson, eds. *Transforming for Stabilization and Reconstruction Operations*. Washington, DC: National Defense University Press, 2003.

Blair, Tony. "Doctrine of the International Community." Speech at the Economic Club of Chicago, Chicago, IL, April 24, 1999. Available at: http://www.pm.gov.uk/output/Page1297.asp.

Boot, Max. "A Mercenary Force for Darfur." *The Wall Street Journal*, October 25, 2006.

Bush, George W. "Address to 2005 World Summit High Level Plenary Meeting," speech given at the United Nations, September 14, 2005.

Center on International Cooperation. *Annual Review of Global Peace Operations 2006*. Bruce Jones, Series editor. London: Lynne Rienner Publishers, 2006.

Deng, Francis M. *Protecting the Dispossessed: A Challenge for the International Community*. Washington, DC: The Brookings Institution, 1993.

De Waal, Alex. "I Will Not Sign." *London Review of Books*. Vol. 28, No. 23, November 30, 2006.

Dobbins, James, Seth G. Jones, Keith Crane, Andrew Rathmell, Brett Steele, Richard Teltschik, and Anga Timilsina. *The UN's Role in Nation Building: From the Congo to Iraq*. Santa Monica: RAND, 2005.

Durch, William J., Victoria K. Holt, Caroline R. Earle, and Moira K. Shanahan. "The Brahimi Report and the Future of UN Peace Operations." Washington, DC: Henry L. Stimson Center, 2003.

Enhancing U.S. Leadership at the United Nations, Report of an Independent Task Force. New York: Council on Foreign Relations, 2002.

Evans, Gareth. "A Rule-Based International Order: Illusory or Achievable?" 2006 CUNY Rustow Memorial Lecture, September 19, 2006.

Feinstein, Lee, "Ban's First UN Test – Darfur," *Los Angeles Times*, January 16, 2007.

Feinstein, Lee. "The 'Responsibility to Protect' Darfuris." *International Herald Tribune*, September 21, 2006.

Feinstein, Lee. "UN-Divided." *The National Interest*. Winter 2005/2006.

Gompert, David C., Courtney Richardson, Richard L. Kugler, and Clifford H. Bernath. "Learning from Darfur: Building a Net-Capable African Force to Stop Mass Killing." Washington, DC: Center for Technology and National Security Policy, July 2005.

Gingrich, Newt and George Mitchell. *American Interests and UN Reform: A Report of the Congressional Task Force on the United Nations*. Washington, DC: United States Institute of Peace, 2005.

Haass, Richard N. and Meghan L. O'Sullivan, eds. *Honey and Vinegar: Incentives, Sanctions, and Foreign Policy*. Washington, DC: Brookings Institution Press, 2000.

Haass, Richard N. *Intervention: The Use of American Military Force in the Post-Cold War World.* Washington, DC: Brookings Institution Press, 1999.

Holt, Victoria K. "The Responsibility to Protect: Considering the Operational Capacity for Civilian Protection." Washington, DC: Henry L. Stimson Center, January 2005 (revised).

Human Security Centre. *Human Security Report 2005: War and Peace in the 21st Century*. New York: Oxford University Press, 2005.

International Commission of Inquiry on Darfur. *Report to the Secretary-General*. Geneva: United Nations, January 25, 2005.

International Commission on Intervention and State Sovereignty. *The Responsibility to Protect*. Ottawa: International Development Research Center, 2001.

International Crisis Group. "Getting the UN into Darfur." *Africa Briefing No. 43*. Nairobi/Brussels, October 12, 2006.

Lindberg, Tod. "Protect the People." *The Washington Times*. September 27, 2005.

Loconte, Joseph. "The Failure to Protect: Lessons from Darfur." *The American Interest*. Vol.2, No. 3 (January/February) 2007.

Luck, Edward C. "Reforming the United Nations: Lessons from a History in Progress." Academic Council on the United Nations Occasional Papers No. 1, 2003.

O'Hanlon, Michael E. *Expanding Global Military Capacity for Humanitarian Intervention.* Washington, DC: Brookings Institution Press, 2003.

Pirnie, Bruce R. and William E. Simons. "Soldiers for Peace: An Operational Typology." Santa Monica, CA: RAND, 1996.

Prunier, Gérard. *Darfur: The Ambiguous Genocide.* Ithaca: Cornell University Press, 2005.

Rieff, David. "Moral Blindness: The Case against Troops for Darfur." *The New Republic.* June 5 and 12, 2006.

Schabas, William A. "Preventing Genocide and Mass Killing: The Challenge for the United Nations." Prepared on behalf of Minority Rights Group International, 2005.

Secretary-General's High-level Panel on Threats, Challenges and Change. *A More Secure World: Our Shared Responsibility.* New York: United Nations, 2004.

U.S. Department of Defense. "Directive Number 3000.05: Military Support for Stability, Security, Transition, and Reconstruction (SSTR) Operations." November 28, 2005.

UN General Assembly and Security Council. *Report of the Panel on United Nations Peace Operations.* Lakhdar Brahimi, Chair. A/55/305-S/2000/809. New York: United Nations, August 21, 2000.

UN Independent Inquiry Committee into the United Nations Oil-for-Food Programme. *Report on the Manipulation of the Oil-for-Food Programme.* New York: United Nations, October 27, 2005.

White House, The. *National Security Strategy of the United States of America.* Washington, DC: September, 2002.

ADVISORY BOARD MEMBERS

Peter Ackerman
ROCKPORT CAPITAL, INC.

Kenneth Anderson
HOOVER INSTITUTION AND
AMERICAN UNIVERSITY

Andrea Bartoli
COLUMBIA UNIVERSITY

Jean Bethke Elshtain
UNIVERSITY OF CHICAGO

Morton H. Halperin
OPEN SOCIETY INSTITUTE

Victoria K. Holt
HENRY L. STIMSON CENTER

Charlotte Ku
AMERICAN SOCIETY OF
INTERNATIONAL LAW

Mark W. Lippert
OFFICE OF SENATOR BARACK OBAMA

Edward C. Luck, *Chair*
COLUMBIA UNIVERSITY

Princeton N. Lyman
COUNCIL ON FOREIGN RELATIONS

Joshua Muravchik
AMERICAN ENTERPRISE INSTITUTE

Diane Orentlicher
AMERICAN UNIVERSITY

Samantha Power
HARVARD UNIVERSITY

Eric Paul Schwartz
UNITED NATIONS DEPUTY SPECIAL
ENVOY FOR TSUNAMI RECOVERY

Anya Schmemann
COUNCIL ON FOREIGN RELATIONS

Andrew J. Shapiro
OFFICE OF SENATOR HILLARY
RODHAM CLINTON

Jennifer J. Simon
SENATE COMMITTEE ON FOREIGN
RELATIONS

Peter W. Singer
THE BROOKINGS INSTITUTION

Gregory H. Stanton
GENOCIDE WATCH

James Traub
THE NEW YORK TIMES MAGAZINE

Joanna Weschler
SECURITY COUNCIL REPORT

William Woodward
THE ALBRIGHT GROUP LLC

ABOUT THE AUTHOR

Lee Feinstein is senior fellow for U.S. foreign policy and international law at the Council on Foreign Relations. Feinstein was senior adviser for peacekeeping and peace enforcement policy in the Office of the Secretary of Defense from 1994–95. He served as member and associate director of the Policy Planning Staff under Secretary of State Warren Christopher and as principal deputy director of policy planning under Secretary of State Madeleine K. Albright. Feinstein served as a human rights adviser on the 2005 congressional Task Force on U.S. Interests and the United Nations, chaired by Newt Gingrich and George Mitchell, and was a principal drafter of the report. He directed the independent task force on *Enhancing U.S. Leadership at the United Nations,* cosponsored by the Council on Foreign Relations and Freedom House in 2002. Feinstein serves on the board of directors of the private Arms Control Association and is a member of the Council on Foreign Relations. He is admitted to the practice of law in New York and Washington, DC.

RECENT COUNCIL SPECIAL REPORTS
SPONSORED BY THE COUNCIL ON FOREIGN RELATIONS

Avoiding Conflict in the Horn of Africa: U.S. Policy Toward Ethiopia and Eritrea
Terrence Lyons; CSR No. 21, November 2006

Living with Hugo: U.S. Policy Toward Hugo Chávez's Venezuela
Richard Lapper; CSR No. 20, November 2006

Reforming U.S. Patent Policy: Getting the Incentives Right
Keith E. Maskus; CSR No. 19, November 2006

Foreign Investment and National Security: Getting the Balance Right
Alan P. Larson and David M. Marchick; CSR No. 18, July 2006

Challenges for a Postelection Mexico
Pamela K. Starr; CSR No. 17, June 2006 (web-only release) and November 2006

U.S.-India Nuclear Cooperation: A Strategy for Moving Forward
Michael A. Levi and Charles D. Ferguson; CSR No. 16, June 2006

Generating Momentum for a New Era in U.S.-Turkey Relations
Steven A. Cook and Elizabeth Sherwood-Randall; CSR No. 15, June 2006

Peace in Papua: Widening a Window of Opportunity
Blair A. King; CSR No. 14, March 2006

Neglected Defense: Mobilizing the Private Sector to Support Homeland Security
Stephen E. Flynn and Daniel B. Prieto; CSR No. 13, March 2006

Afghanistan's Uncertain Transition From Turmoil to Normalcy
Barnett R. Rubin; CSR No. 12, March 2006

Preventing Catastrophic Nuclear Terrorism
Charles D. Ferguson; CSR No. 11, March 2006

Getting Serious About the Twin Deficits
Menzie D. Chinn; CSR No. 10, September 2005

Both Sides of the Aisle: A Call for Bipartisan Foreign Policy
Nancy E. Roman; CSR No. 9, September 2005

Forgotten Intervention? What the United States Needs to Do in the Western Balkans
Amelia Branczik and William L. Nash; CSR No. 8, June 2005

A New Beginning: Strategies for a More Fruitful Dialogue with the Muslim World
Craig Charney and Nicole Yakatan; CSR No. 7, May 2005

Power-Sharing in Iraq
David L. Phillips; CSR No. 6, April 2005

To purchase a printed copy, call the Brookings Institution Press: 800-537-5487.
Note: Council Special Reports are available to download from the Council's website, CFR.org.
For more information, contact publications@cfr.org.